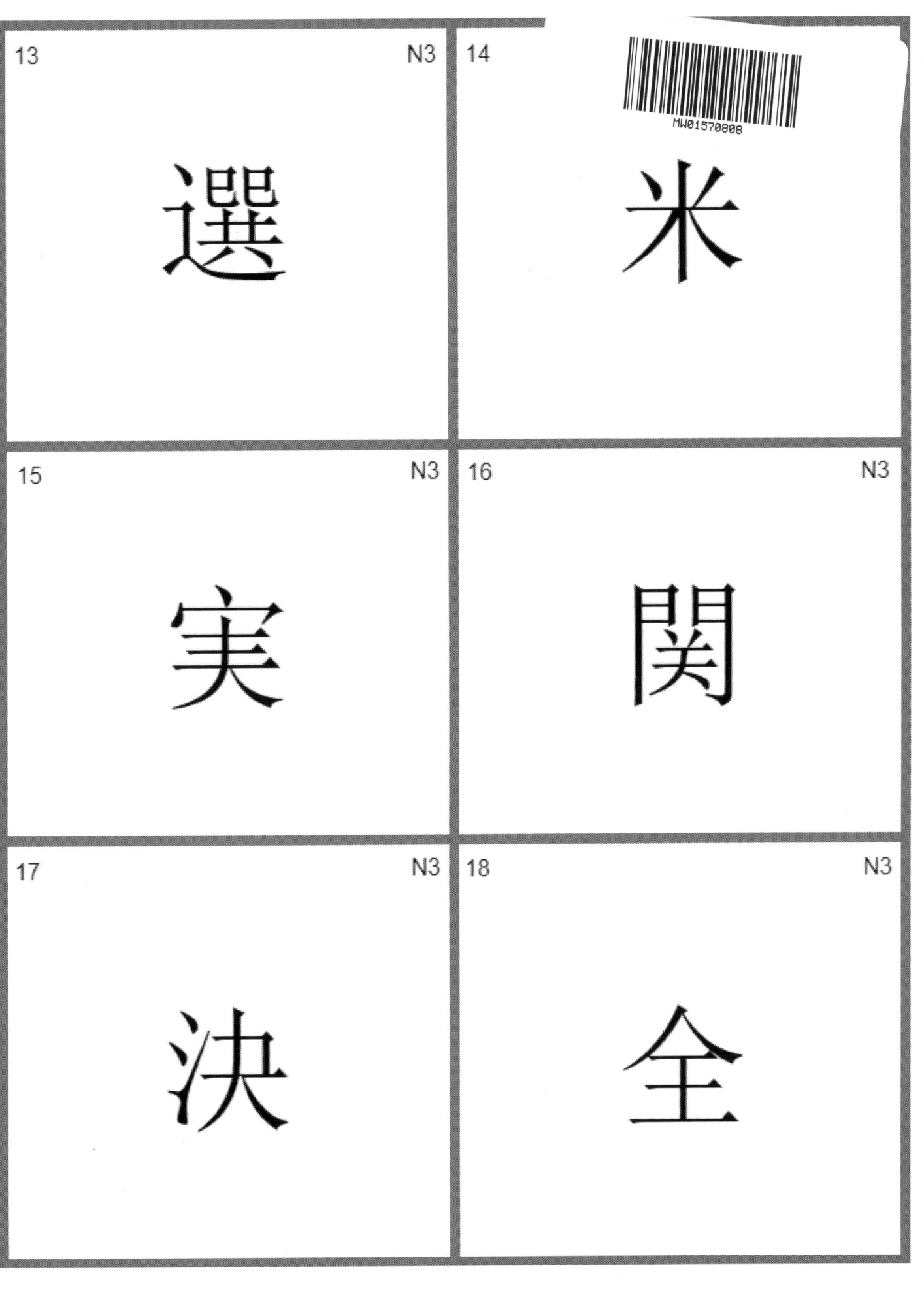

13 N3	14 N3
えら.ぶ, セン, elect, select, choose, prefer	こめ, ベイ, マイ, メエトル, ヨ, rice, USA, metre

15 N3	16 N3
み, みの.る, まこと, まことに, みの, ジツ, シツ, ミチ, reality, truth	せき, -ぜき, かか.わる, からくり, かんぬき, カン, connection, barrier, gateway, involve, concerning

17 N3	18 N3
き.める, -ぎ.め, き.まる, さ.く, ケツ, decide, fix, agree upon, appoint	まった.く, すべ.て, ゼン, whole, entire, all, complete, fulfill

19 N3	20 N3
表	戦

21 N3	22 N3
経	最

23 N3	24 N3
現	調

19 N3	20 N3
おもて, -おもて, あらわ.す, あらわ.れる, あら.わす, ヒョウ, surface, table, chart, diagram	いくさ, たたか.う, おのの.く, そよ.く, わなな.く, セン, ワナナ, war, battle, match

21 N3	22 N3
へ.る, た.つ, たていと, はか.る, のり, ケイ, キョウ, sutra, longitude, pass thru, expire, warp	もっと.も, つま, サイ, シュ, utmost, most, extreme

23 N3	24 N3
あらわ.れる, あらわ.す, うつつ, うつ.つ, ゲン, present, existing, actual	しら.べる, しら.べ, ととの.う, チョウ, トトノ.エ, tune, tone, meter, key (music), writing style, prepare, exorcise, investigate

25 N3 ば.ける, ば.かす, ふ.ける, け.する, カ, ケ, change, take the form of, influence, enchant, delude, -ization	**26** N3 あ.たる, あ.たり, あ.てる, あ.て, まさ.に, まさ.にべし, トウ, hit, right, appropriate, himself
27 N3 ヤク, promise, approximately, shrink	**28** N3 くび, シュ, neck
29 N3 のり, ホウ, ハッ, ホッ, フラン, method, law, rule, principle, model, system	**30** N3 さが, セイ, ショウ, sex, gender, nature

31 要	32 制
33 治	34 務
35 成	36 期

31 N3	32 N3
い.る, かなめ, ヨウ, need, main point, essence, pivot, key to	セイ, system, law, rule

33 N3	34 N3
おさ.める, おさ.まる, なお.る, ジ, チ, ナオ, reign, be at peace, calm down, subdue, quell, govt, cure, heal, rule, conserve	つと.め ム, task, duties

35 N3	36 N3
な.る, な.す, セイ, ジョウ, -ナ, turn into, become, get, grow, elapse, reach	キ, ゴ, period, time, date, term

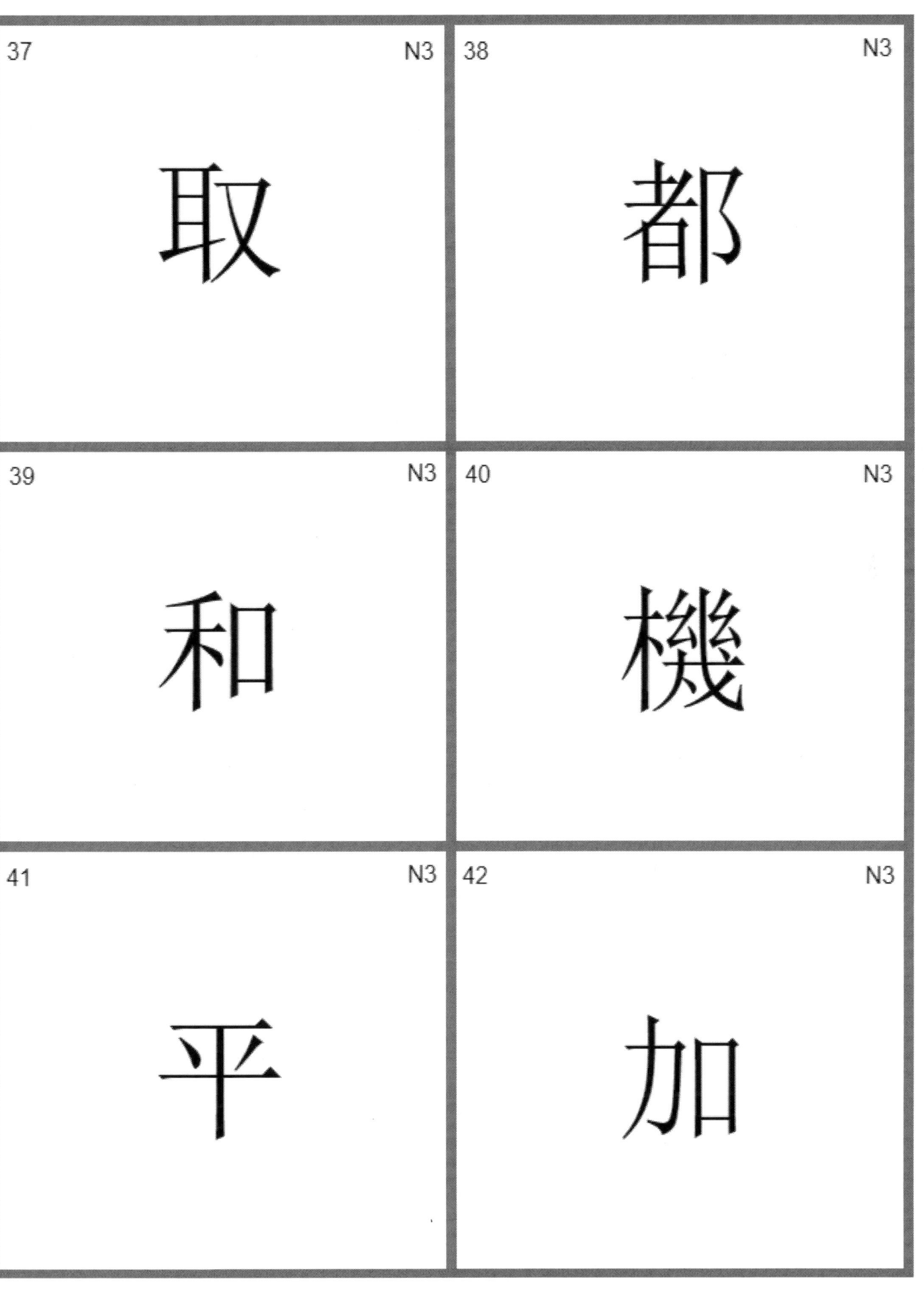

37 N3 と.る, と.り, と.り-, とり, -ど.り, シュ, take, fetch, take up	**38** N3 みやこ, ト, ツ, metropolis, capital
39 N3 やわ.らぐ やわ.らげる なご.む ワ オ カ ナゴ.ヤ harmony, Japanese style, peace, soften, Japan	**40** N3 はた キ mechanism, opportunity, occasion, machine, airplane
41 N3 たい.ら -だいら ひら ひら ヘイ ビョウ ヒョウ even, flat, peace	**42** N3 くわ.える くわ.わる カ add, addition, increase, join, include, Canada

43 受	44 続
45 進	46 数
47 記	48 初

43 N3	44 N3
う.ける -う.け ジュ ウ.カ accept, undergo, answer (phone), take, get, catch, receive	つづ.く つづ.ける ゾク ショク コウ キョウ ツグ.ナ continue, series, sequel

45 N3	46 N3
すす.む シン スス.メ advance, proceed, progress, promote	かず かぞ.える しばしば せ.める スウ ス サク ソク シュ ワズラワ.シ number, strength, fate, law, figures

47 N3	48 N3
キ シル. scribe, account, narrative	はじ.め はじ.めて はつ はつ- うい- -そ.める ショ -ゾ. first time, beginning

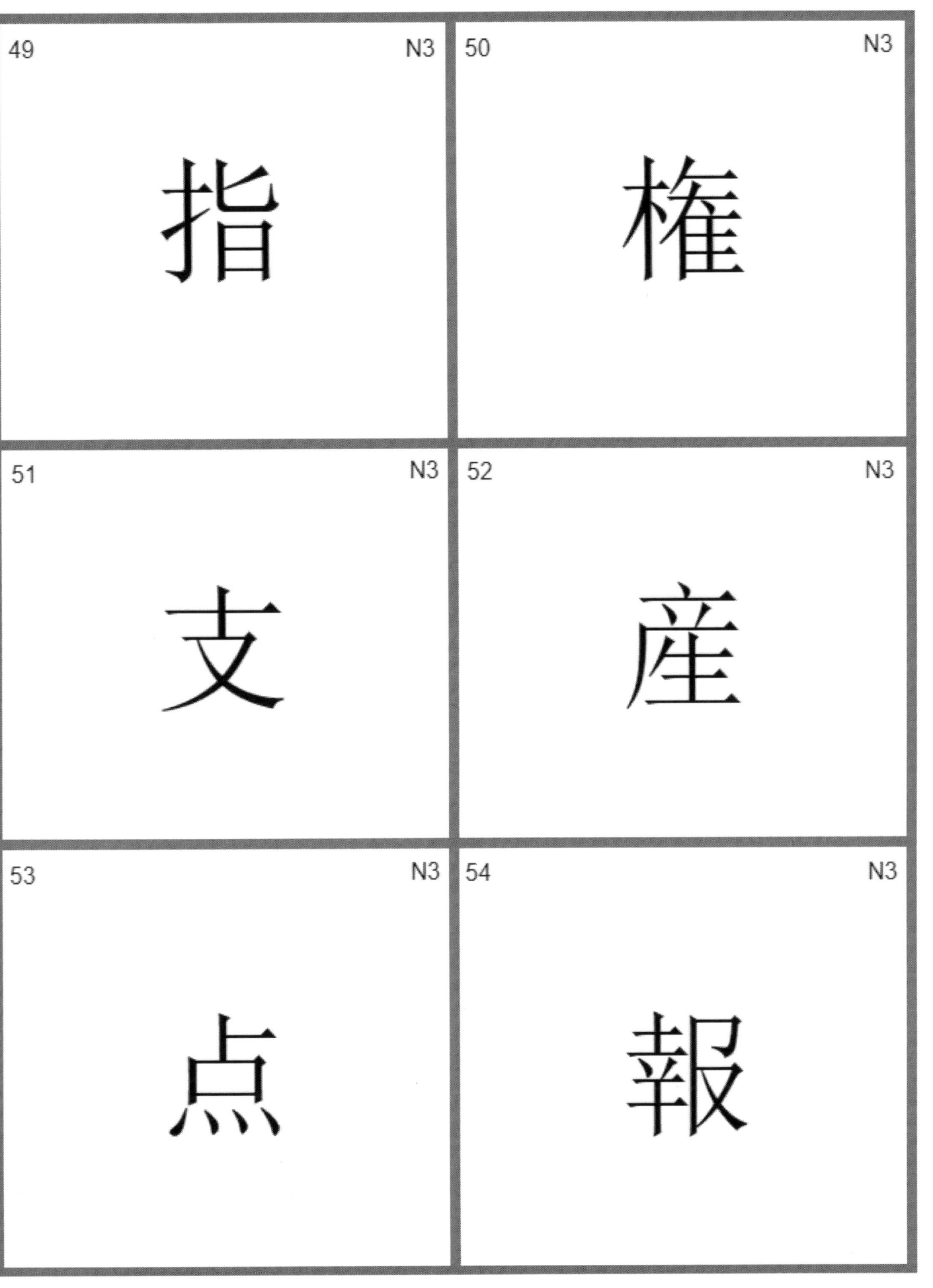

49 N3 ゆび さ.す シ -サ. finger, point to, indicate, put into, play (chess), measure (ruler)	**50** N3 おもり かり はか.る ケン ゴン authority, power, rights
51 N3 しんよう じゅうまた branch, support, sustain	**52** N3 う.む う.まれる うぶ- サン ム. products, bear, give birth, yield, childbirth, native, property
53 N3 つ.ける つ.く た.てる さ.す と ぼ.す と も.す ぼち テン spot, point, mark, speck, decimal point	**54** N3 むく.いる ホウ report, news, reward, retribution

55 N3	56 N3
済	活

57 N3	58 N3
原	共

59 N3	60 N3
得	解

55 N3	56 N3
す.む -ず.み -ずみ す.まない す.ます -す.ます すく.う な.す わたし サイ セイ ワタ. finish, come to an end, excusable, need not	い.きる い.かす い.ける カツ lively, resuscitation, being helped, living
57 N3	58 N3
ゲン ハ meadow, original, primitive, field, plain, prairie, tundra, wilderness	とも とも.に -ども キョウ together, both, neither, all, and, alike, with
59 N3	60 N3
え.る トク ウ. gain, get, find, earn, acquire, can, may, able to, profit, advantage, benefit	と.く と.かす と.ける ほど.く ほど.ける わか.る カイ ゲ サト. unravel, notes, key, explanation, understanding, untie, undo, solve, answer, cancel, absolve, explain, minute

61 N3	62 N3
まじ.わる まじ.える ま.じる まじ.る ま.ざる ま.ぜる -か.う か.わす かわ.す コウ コモゴ mingle, mixing, association, coming & going	シ assets, resources, capital, funds, data, be conducive to, contribute to

63 N3	64 N3
あらかじ.め ヨ シャ beforehand, previous, myself, I	む.く む.い -む.き む.ける -む.け む.かう む.かい む.こう む.こう- むこ コウ ムカ. yonder, facing, beyond, confront, defy, tend toward, approach

65 N3	66 N3
きわ サイ -ギ occasion, side, edge, verge, dangerous, adventurous, indecent, time, when	か.つ -が.ち まさ.る すぐ.れる ショウ カ victory, win, prevail, excel

67 面	68 告
69 反	70 判
71 認	72 参

67 N3	68 N3
おも おもて メン ベン ツ mask, face, features, surface	コク ツ.ゲ revelation, tell, inform, announce

69 N3	70 N3
そ.る そ.らす かえ.す かえ.る ハン ホン タン ホ -カエ. anti-	わか.る ハン バン judgement, signature, stamp, seal

71 N3	72 N3
みと.める したた.める ニン acknowledge, witness, discern, recognize, appreciate, believe	まい.る まい- まじわる サン シン ミ nonplussed, three, going, coming, visiting, visit, be defeated, die, be madly in love

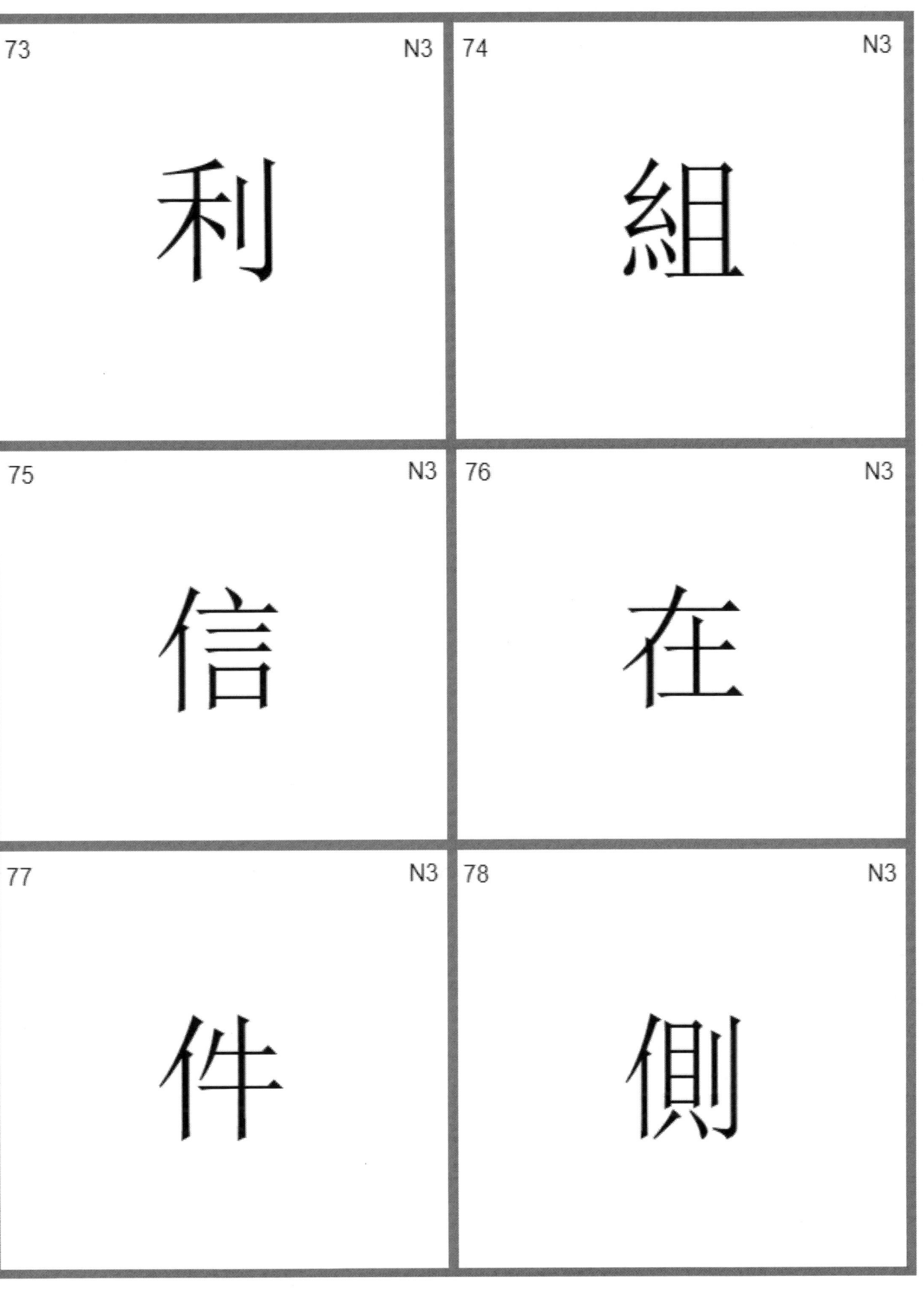

73 N3	74 N3
リ キ. profit, advantage, benefit	く.む くみ -ぐみ ソ association, braid, plait, construct, assemble, unite, cooperate, grapple
75 N3	76 N3
シ faith, truth, fidelity, trust	ザイ ア. exist, outskirts, suburbs, located in
77 N3	78 N3
くだん ケン affair, case, matter, item	かわ がわ そば ソク side, lean, oppose, regret

79 任	80 引
81 求	82 所
83 次	84 昨

79 N3 まか.せる ニン マカ. responsibility, duty, term, entrust to, appoint	**80** N3 ひ.く ひ.き ひ.き- -び.き イン ヒ.ケ pull, tug, jerk, admit, install, quote, refer to
81 N3 もと.める キュウ グ request, want, wish for, require, demand	**82** N3 ところ -ところ どころ ショ ト place
83 N3 つ.ぐ ジ シ ツ next, order, sequence	**84** N3 サク yesterday, previous

85 N3	86 N3
論	官

87 N3	88 N3
増	係

89 N3	90 N3
感	情

85 　　　　　　　　　　N3 ロン argument, discourse	86 　　　　　　　　　　N3 カン bureaucrat, the government
87 　　　　　　　　　　N3 ま.す ま.し ふ.える ゾウ フ.ヤ increase, add, augment, gain, promote	88 　　　　　　　　　　N3 かか.る かかり -がかり かか.わる ケイ person in charge, connection, duty, concern oneself
89 　　　　　　　　　　N3 カン emotion, feeling, sensation	90 　　　　　　　　　　N3 なさ.け ジョウ セイ feelings, emotion, passion, sympathy, circumstances, facts

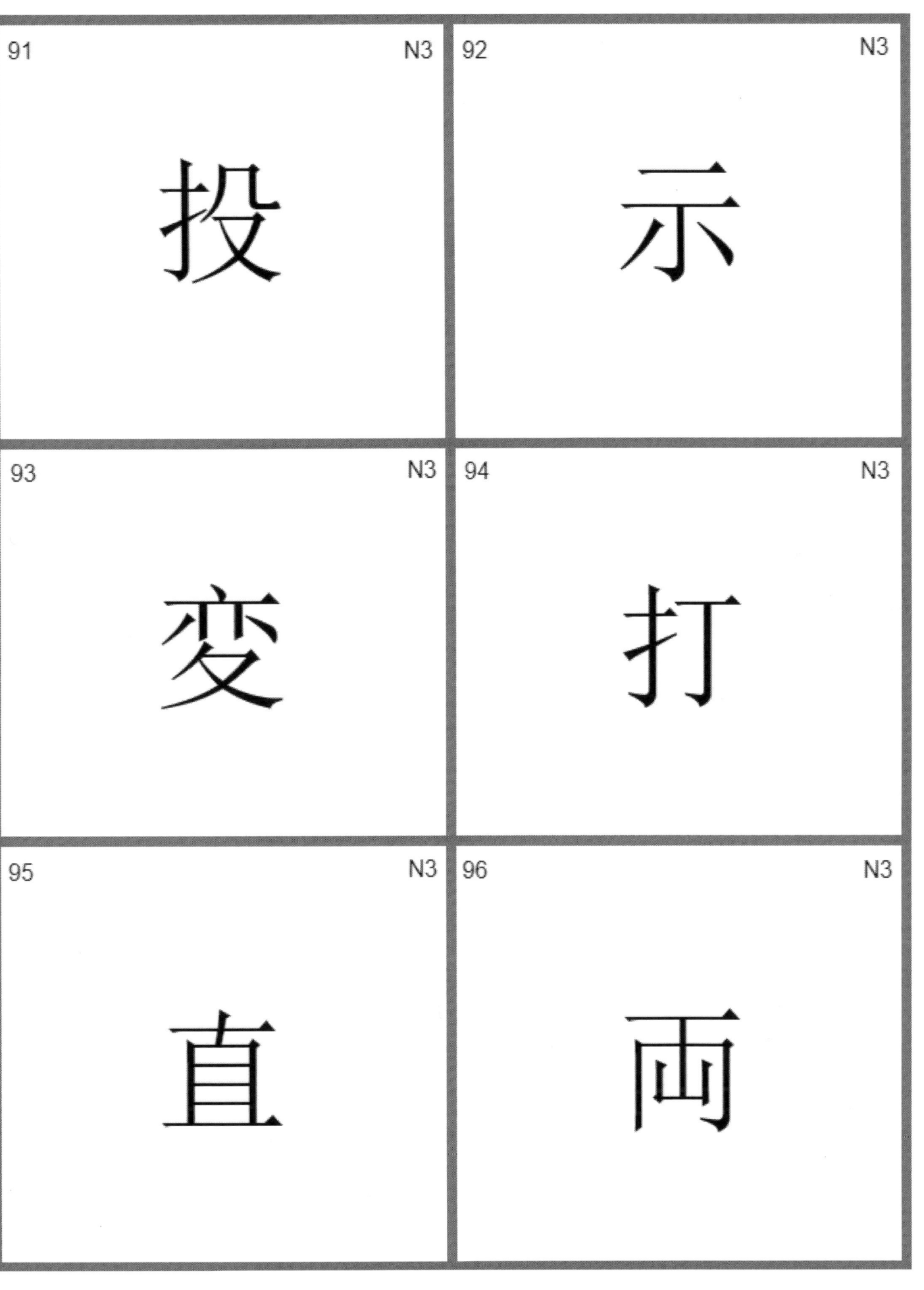

91 N3 な.げる -な.げ トウ throw, discard, abandon, launch into, join, invest in, hurl, give up, sell at a loss	**92** N3 しめ.す ジ シ show, indicate, point out, express, display
93 N3 か.わる か.わり か.える ヘン unusual, change, strange	**94** N3 う.つ う.ち- ダ ダアス ブ. strike, hit, knock, pound, dozen
95 N3 ただ.ちに なお.す -なお.す なお.る なお.き チョク ジキ ジカ ス. straightaway, honesty, frankness, fix, repair	**96** N3 てる リョウ フタ both, old Japanese coin, counter for vehicles, two

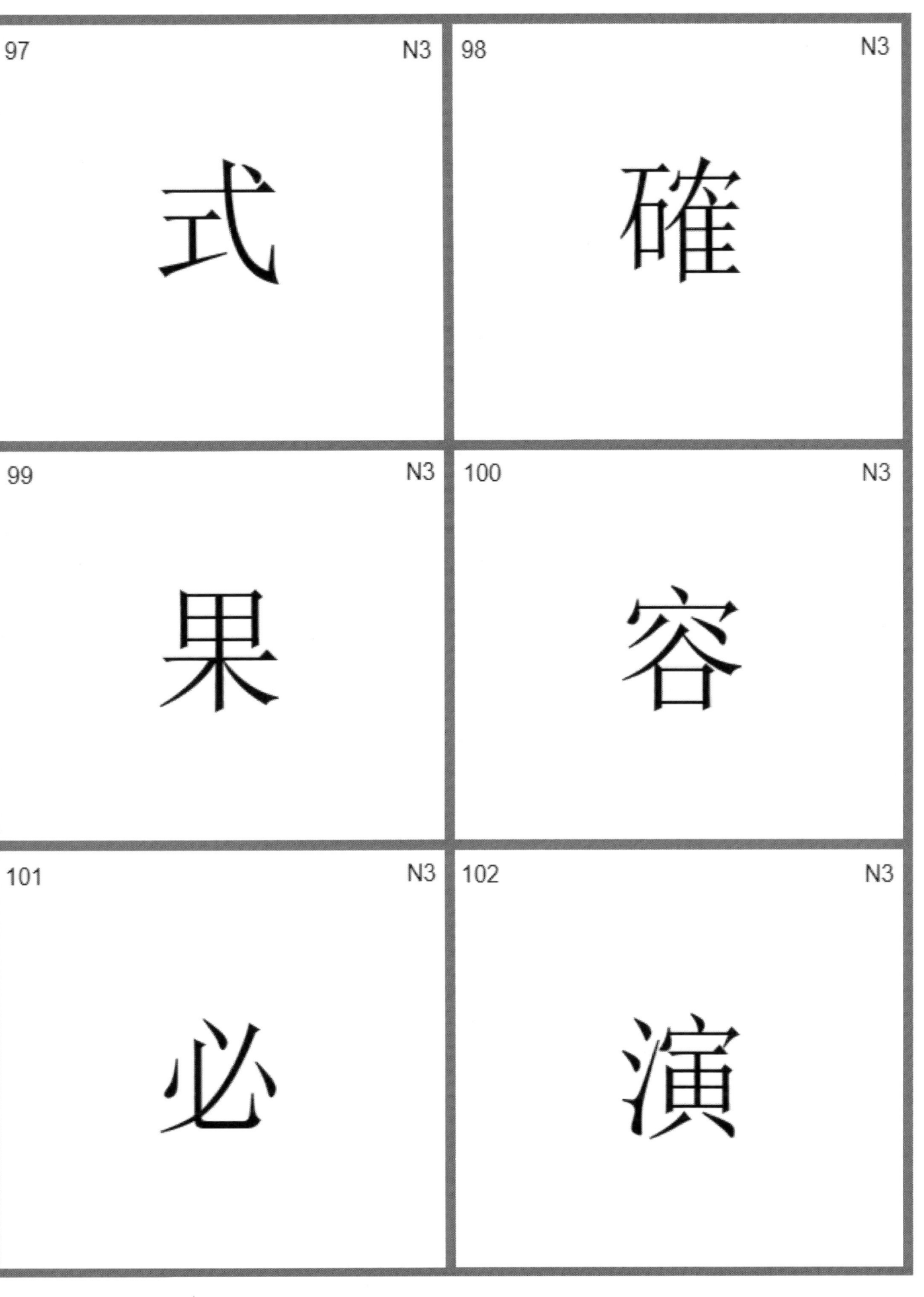

97 N3	98 N3
シ style, ceremony, rite, function, method, system, form, expression	たし.か たし.かめる カク コウ assurance, firm, tight, hard, solid, confirm, clear, evident

99 N3	100 N3
は.たす はた.す -は.たす は.てる -は.てる カ ハ. fruit, reward, carry out, achieve, complete, end, finish, succeed	ヨウ イ.レ contain, form, looks

101 N3	102 N3
かなら.ず ヒツ invariably, certain, inevitable	エン performance, act, play, render, stage

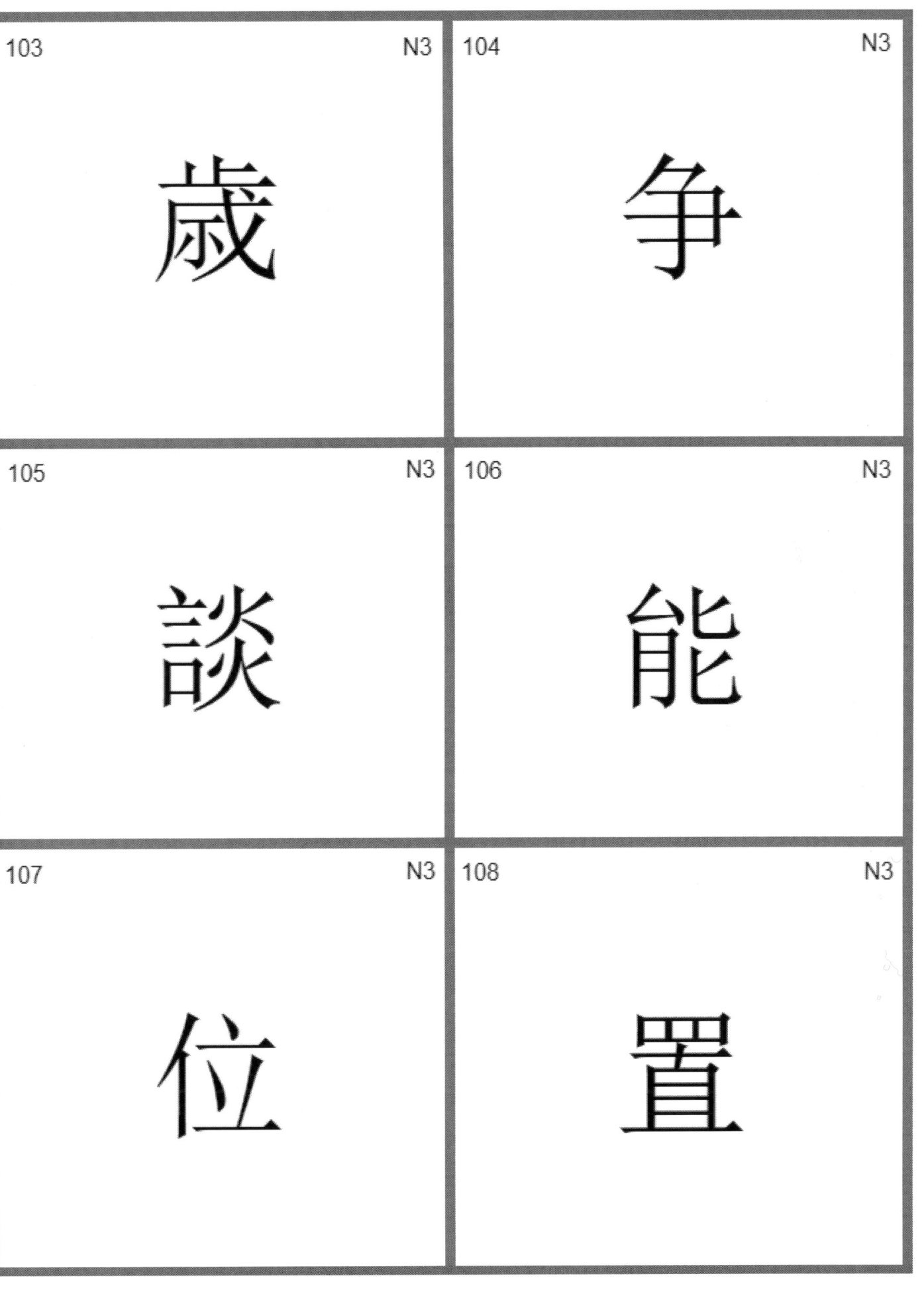

103 N3	104 N3
とし とせ よわい サイ セイ year-end, age, occasion, opportunity	あらそ.う いか.で か ソウ contend, dispute, argue
105 N3	106 N3
ダン discuss, talk	ノウ ヨ. ability, talent, skill, capacity
107 N3	108 N3
くらい イ グラ rank, grade, throne, crown, about, some	お.く チ -オ. placement, put, set, deposit, leave behind, keep, employ, pawn

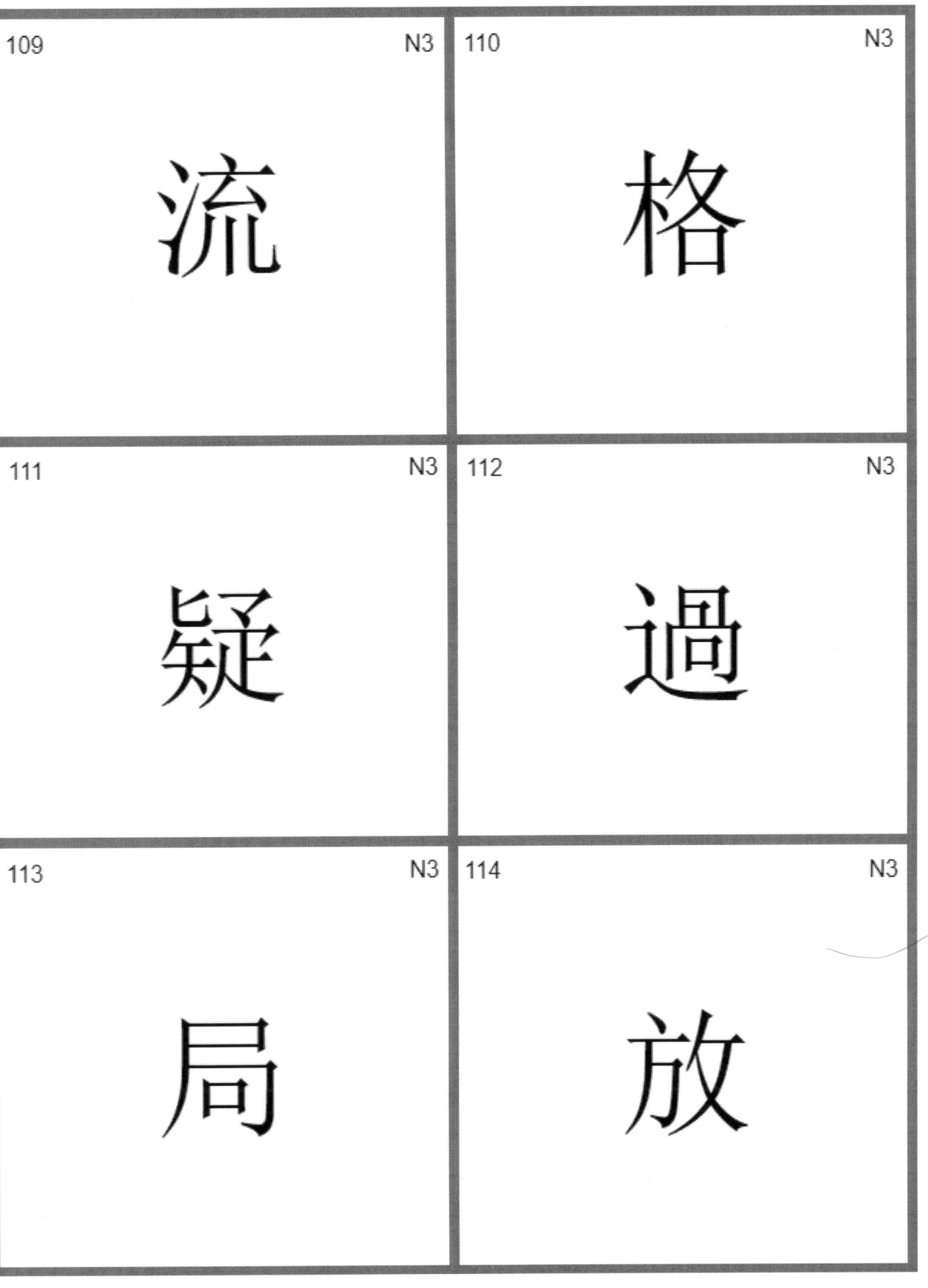

109 N3 なが.れる なが.れ なが.す リュウ ル -ナガ. current, a sink, flow, forfeit	**110** N3 カク コウ キャク ゴ status, rank, capacity, character, case (law, grammar)
111 N3 うたが.う ギ doubt, distrust, be suspicious, question	**112** N3 す.ぎる -す.ぎる -す.ぎ す.ごす あやま.つ あやま.ち カ overdo, exceed, go beyond, error
113 N3 つぼね キョク bureau, board, office, affair, conclusion, court lady, lady-in-waiting, her apartment	**114** N3 はな.す -っぱな.し はな.つ はな.れる こ.く ホウ ホウ. set free, release, fire, shoot, emit, banish, liberate

115　　　　　　　　N3 常	116　　　　　　　　N3 状
117　　　　　　　　N3 球	118　　　　　　　　N3 職
119　　　　　　　　N3 与	120　　　　　　　　N3 供

115 N3 つね とこ ジョウ usual, ordinary, normal, regular	**116** N3 ジョウ status quo, conditions, circumstances, form, appearance
117 N3 キュウ タ ball, sphere	**118** N3 ショク ソ post, employment, work
119 N3 あた.える あずか.る くみ.する ヨ ト モ bestow, participate in, give, award, impart, provide, cause, gift, godsend	**120** N3 そな.える とも -ども キョウ ク クウ グ submit, offer, present, serve (meal), accompany

121 N3	122 N3
役	構

123 N3	124 N3
割	費

125 N3	126 N3
付	由

121 N3	122 N3
ヤク エ duty, war, campaign, drafted labor, office, service, role	かま.える コウ カマ. posture, build, pretend
123 N3	124 N3
わ.る わり わ.り わ.れる さ.く カツ proportion, comparatively, divide, cut, separate, split	つい.やす つい.える ヒ expense, cost, spend, consume, waste
125 N3	126 N3
つ.ける -つ.ける -づ.ける つ.け つ.け- -つ.け -づ.け -づけ つ.く -づ.く つ.き -つ.き -つフ -ヅ adhere, attach, refer to, append	よし よ.る ユ ユウ ユイ wherefore, a reason

127 N3	128 N3
説	難
129 N3	130 N3
優	夫
131 N3	132 N3
収	断

127 N3	128 N3
セツ ゼイ ト. rumor, opinion, theory	かた.い -がた.い むずか.しい むづか.しい むつか.しい ナン -ニク. difficult, impossible, trouble, accident, defect
129 N3	130 N3
やさ.しい すぐ.れる ユウ ウ マサ. tenderness, excel, surpass, actor, superiority, gentleness	おっと フ フウ ブ ソ. husband, man
131 N3	132 N3
おさ.める シュウ オサ.マ income, obtain, reap, pay, supply, store	た.つ ことわ.る さだ.める ダン severance, decline, refuse, apologize, warn, dismiss, prohibit, decision, judgement, cutting

133 N3	134 N3
石	違

135 N3	136 N3
消	神

137 N3	138 N3
番	規

133 N3 セキ シャク コク イ stone	134 N3 ちが.う ちが.い ちが.える -ちが.える たが.う たが.える イ difference, differ
135 N3 き.える け.す ショウ extinguish, blow out, turn off, neutralize, cancel	136 N3 かみ かん- こう シン ジン gods, mind, soul
137 N3 バン ツガ. turn, number in a series	138 N3 キ standard, measure

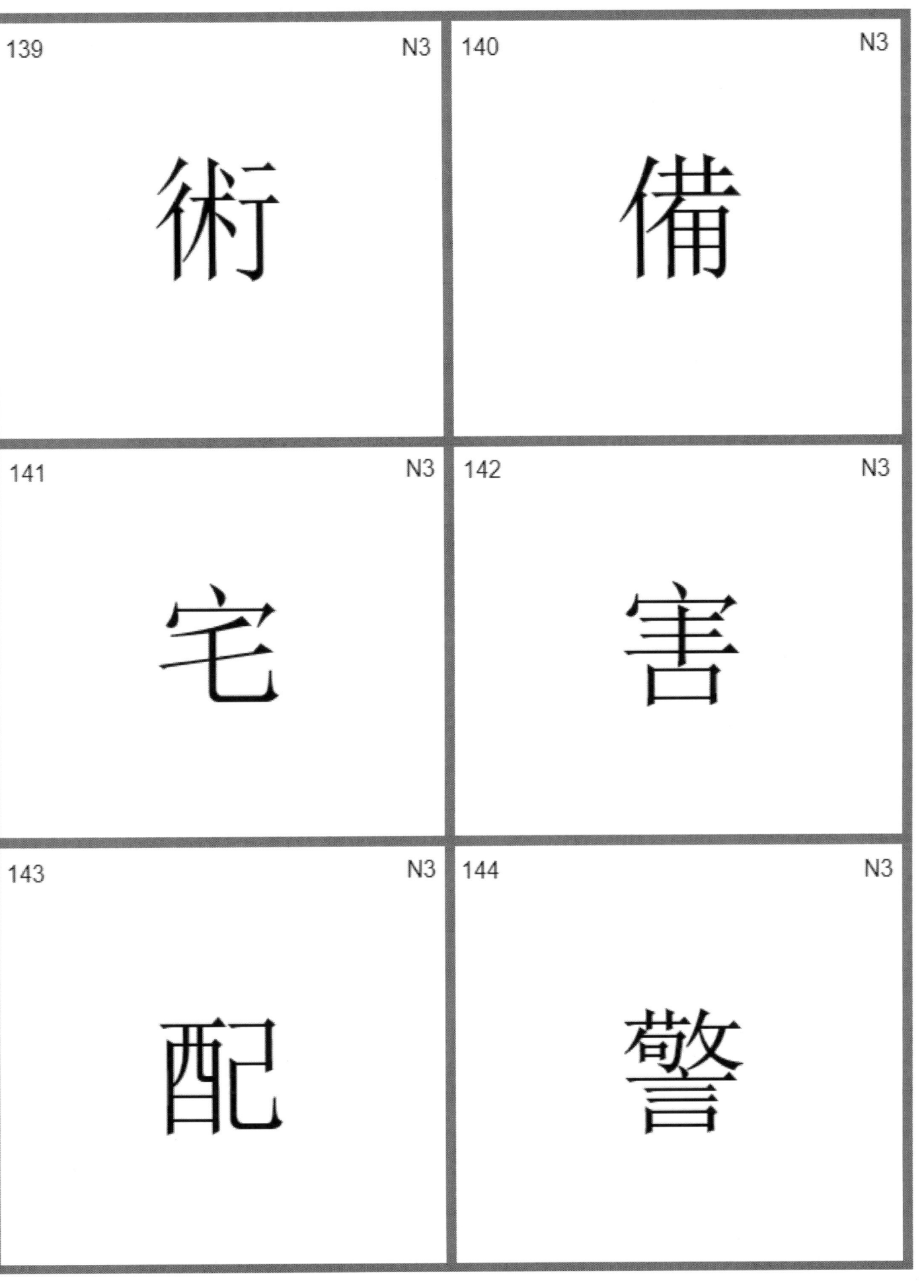

139 N3	140 N3
すべ ジュツ art, technique, skill, means, trick, resources, magic	そな.える そな.わる ビ ツブサ. equip, provision, preparation

141 N3	142 N3
タ home, house, residence, our house, my husband	ガイ harm, injury

143 N3	144 N3
くば.る ハイ distribute, spouse, exile, rationing	いまし.める ケイ admonish, commandment

145 N3	146 N3
育	席

147 N3	148 N3
訪	乗

149 N3	150 N3
残	想

145 N3	146 N3
そだ.つ そだ.ち そだ.てる イク ハグク. bring up, grow up, raise, rear	むしろ セキ seat, mat, occasion, place
147 N3	148 N3
おとず.れる たず.ねる ホウト. call on, visit, look up, offer sympathy	の.る -の.り ジョウ ショウ ノ.セ ride, power, multiplication, record, counter for vehicles, board, mount, join
149 N3	150 N3
のこ.る のこ.す そこな.う のこ.り ザン サン remainder, leftover, balance	おも.う ソウ ソ concept, think, idea, thought

151 N3	152 N3
声	念 |//
153 N3	154 N3
助	労
155 N3	156 N3
例	然

151 N3 こえ こわ- セイ ショウ voice	152 N3 ネン wish, sense, idea, thought, feeling, desire, attention
153 N3 たす.ける たす.かる す.ける すけ ジョ help, rescue, assist	154 N3 ろう.する いたわ.る いた.ずき ねぎら つか.れる ねぎら.う ロウ labor, thank for, reward for, toil, trouble
155 N3 たと.える レイ example, custom, usage, precedent	156 N3 しか しか.り しか.し さ ゼン ネン sort of thing, so, if so, in that case, well

157 N3	158 N3
限	追

159 N3	160 N3
商	葉

161 N3	162 N3
伝	働

157 N3 かぎ.る かぎ.り -かぎ.り ゲン limit, restrict, to best of ability	158 N3 ツイ オ. chase, drive away, follow, pursue, meanwhile
159 N3 ショウ アキナ. make a deal, selling, dealing in, merchant	160 N3 ヨウ leaf, plane, lobe, needle, blade, spear, counter for flat things, fragment, piece
161 N3 つた.わる つた.える つた.う つだ.う -づた.い デン テン ツ transmit, go along, walk along, follow, report, communicate, legend, tradition	162 N3 はたら.く ドウ リュク リキ ロク リョク work, (kokuji)

163 N3	164 N3
形	景

165 N3	166 N3
落	好

167 N3	168 N3
退	頭

163 N3	164 N3
かた -がた かたち ケイ ギョウ ナ shape, form, style	ケ scenery, view

165 N3	166 N3
お.ちる お.ち ラク オ.ト fall, drop, come down	この.む す.く よ.い コウ イ. fond, pleasing, like something

167 N3	168 N3
しりぞ.く しりぞ.ける ひ.く の.く の.ける ど.く タイ retreat, withdraw, retire, resign, repel, expel, reject	あたま かしら -がしら トウ ズ ト カブ head, counter for large animals

169 N3	170 N3
負	渡

171 N3	172 N3
失	差

173 N3	174 N3
末	守

169 N3 ま.ける ま.かす お.う フ defeat, negative, -, minus, bear, owe, assume a responsibility	**170** N3 わた.る -わた.る ト ワタ. transit, ford, ferry, cross, import, deliver, diameter, migrate
171 N3 うしな.う う.せる シツ lose, error, fault, disadvantage, loss	**172** N3 さ.す さ.し サ distinction, difference, variation, discrepancy, margin, balance
173 N3 すえ マツ バツ end, close, tip, powder, posterity	**174** N3 まも.る まも.り もり -もり シュ ス カ guard, protect, defend, obey

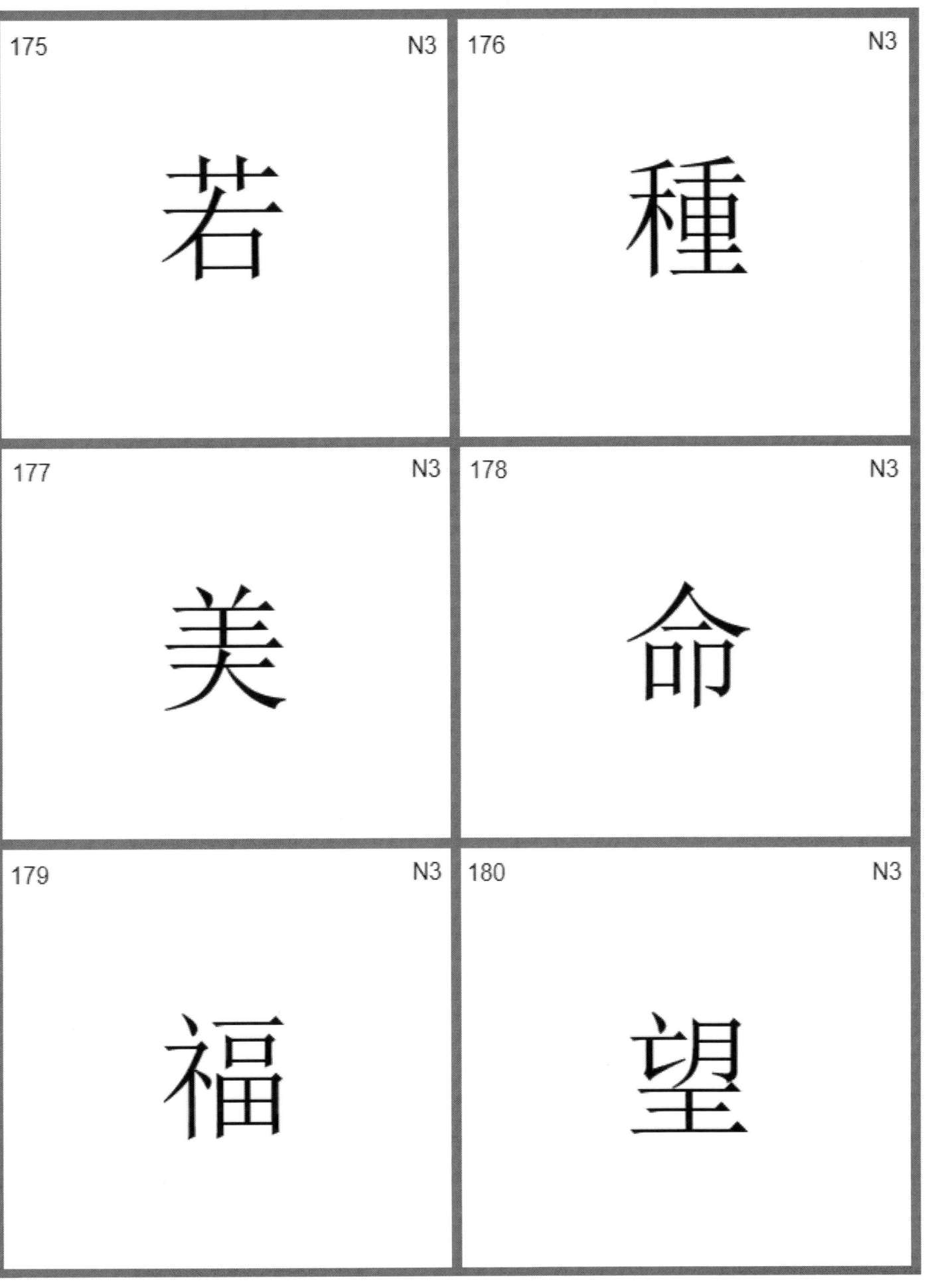

175 N3	176 N3
わか.い わか- も.しくわ も.し ジャク ニャク ニャモ.シク young, if, perhaps, possibly, low number, immature	たね シュ -グ species, kind, class, variety, seed

177 N3	178 N3
ビ ミ ウツク.シ beauty, beautiful	いのち メイ ミョウ fate, command, decree, destiny, life, appoint

179 N3	180 N3
フ blessing, fortune, luck, wealth	のぞ.む ボウ モウ モ ambition, full moon, hope, desire, aspire to, expect

181 N3	182 N3
非	観

183 N3	184 N3
察	段

185 N3	186 N3
横	深

181 N3 あら.ず ヒ un-, mistake, negative, injustice, non-	182 N3 み.る しめ.す カン outlook, look, appearance, condition, view
183 N3 サツ guess, presume, surmise, judge, understand	184 N3 ダン タン grade, steps, stairs
185 N3 よこ オウ sideways, side, horizontal, width, woof	186 N3 ふか.い -ぶか.い ふか.まる ふか.める み- シン deep, heighten, intensify, strengthen

187 　　　　N3 申	188 　　　　N3 様
189 　　　　N3 財	190 　　　　N3 港
191 　　　　N3 識	192 　　　　N3 呼

187 N3 もう.す もう.し- さる シン have the honor to, sign of the monkey, 3-5PM, ninth sign of Chinese zodiac	**188** N3 さま さん ヨウ ショウ Esq., way, manner, situation, polite suffix
189 N3 ザイ サイ ゾ property, money, wealth, assets	**190** N3 みなと コウ harbor
191 N3 シ discriminating, know, write	**192** N3 コ ヨ. call, call out to, invite

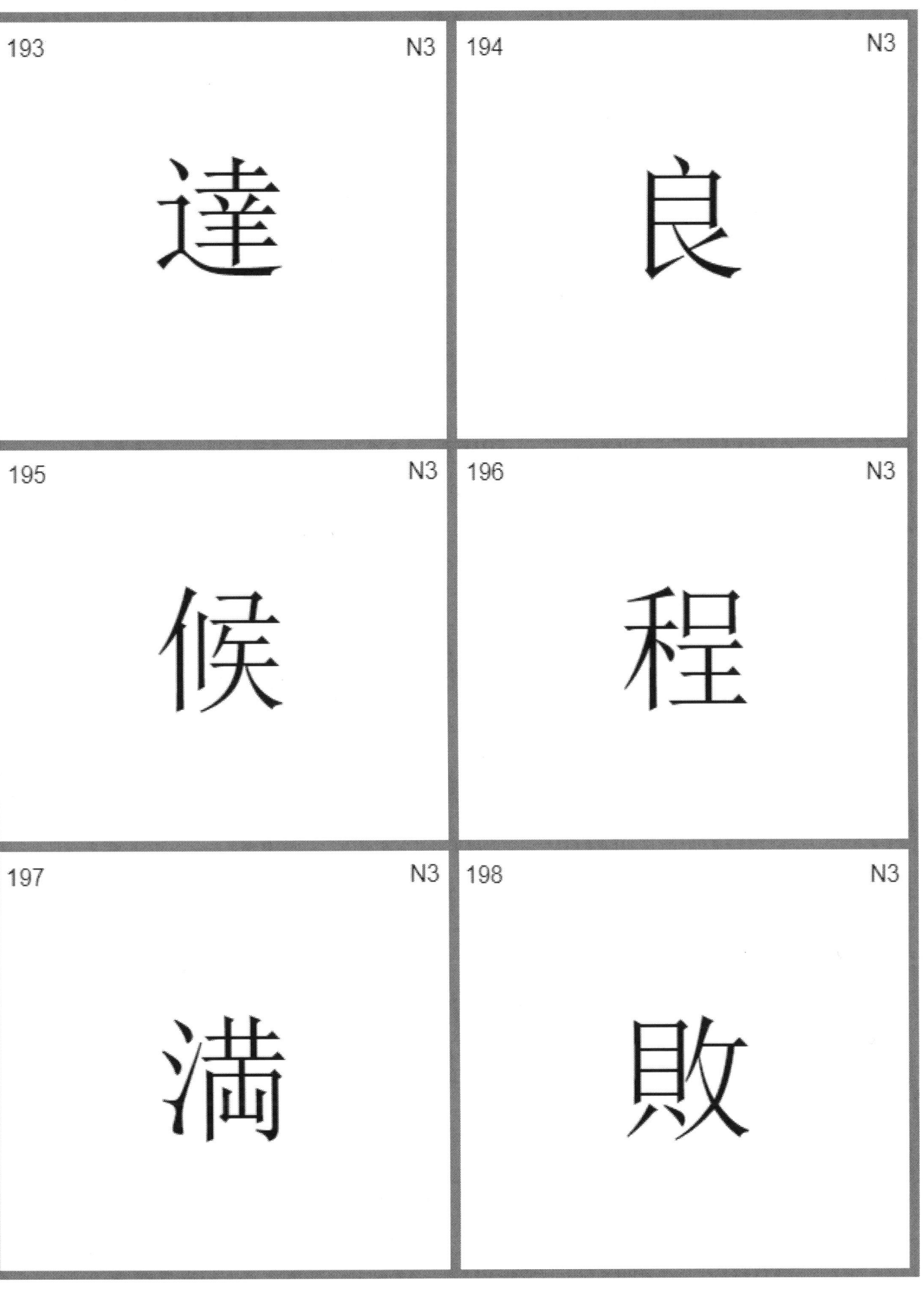

193 N3 タツ ダ -タ accomplished, reach, arrive, attain	194 N3 よ.い -よ.い い.いリョウ -イ. good, pleasing, skilled
195 N3 そうろうコウ climate, season, weather	196 N3 ほどテイ -ホ extent, degree, law, formula, distance, limits, amount
197 N3 み.ちる み.つマン バン ミ.タ full, enough, pride, satisfy	198 N3 やぶ.れるハイ failure, defeat, reversal

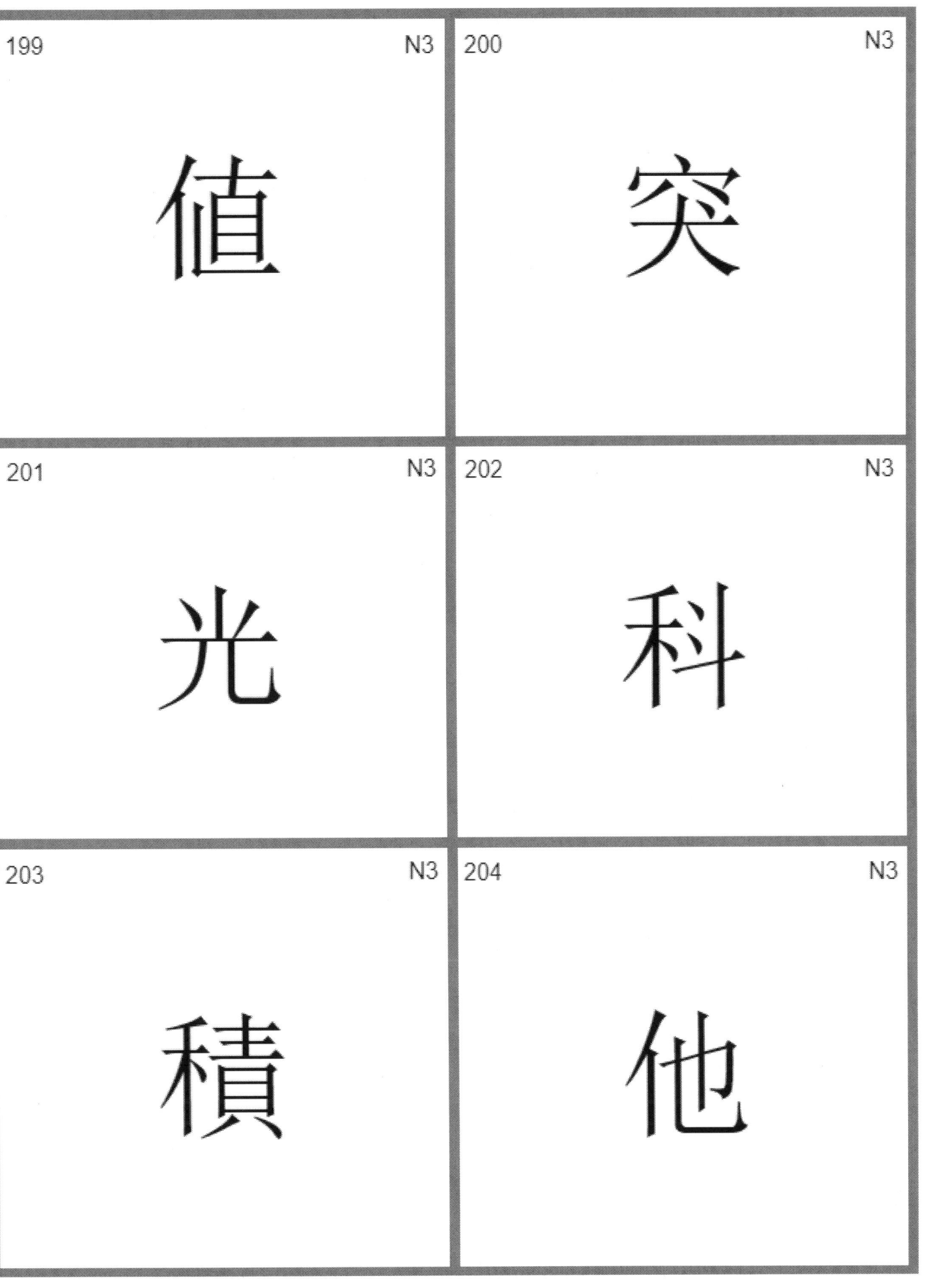

199 N3 ねチ アタ price, cost, value	200 N3 つ.く トツ カ stab, protruding, thrusting, thrust, pierce, prick
201 N3 ひか.る コウ ヒカ ray, light	202 N3 カ department, course, section
203 N3 つ.む -づ.み つ.もる セキ ツ.モ volume, product (x*y), acreage, contents, pile up, stack, load, amass	204 N3 ほか タ other, another, the others

205　　N3	206　　N3
処	太

207　　N3	208　　N3
客	否

209　　N3	210　　N3
師	登

205 N3	206 N3
ところ -こ お.る ショ dispose, manage, deal with, sentence, condemn, act, behave, place	ふと.い タイ タ フト. plump, thick, big around
207 N3	208 N3
キャク カク guest, visitor, customer, client	いな いや ヒ negate, no, noes, refuse, decline, deny
209 N3	210 N3
いくさ シ expert, teacher, master, army, war	のぼ.る トウ ト ドウ ショウ チョウ ア.ガ ascend, climb up

211 N3	212 N3
易	速

213 N3	214 N3
存	飛

215 N3	216 N3
殺	号

211 N3 やさ.しい やす.い エキ イ easy, ready to, simple, fortune-telling, divination	212 N3 はや.い はや- はや.める ソク スミ.ヤ quick, fast
213 N3 ソン ゾ suppose, be aware of, believe, feel	214 N3 と.ぶ と.ばす ヒ -ト.バ fly, skip (pages), scatter
215 N3 ころ.す -ごろ.し そ.ぐ サツ サイ セツ kill, murder, butcher, slice off, split, diminish, reduce, spoil	216 N3 さけ.ぶ よびな ゴウ nickname, number, item, title, pseudonym, name, call

217 N3	218 N3
単	座
219 N3	220 N3
破	除
221 N3	222 N3
完	降

217 N3	218 N3
ひとえ タン simple, one, single, merely	すわ.る ザ squat, seat, cushion, gathering, sit
219 N3	220 N3
やぶ.る ハ ヤブ.レ rend, rip, tear, break, destroy, defeat, frustrate	のぞ.く -よ.け ジョ ジ exclude, division (x, ÷), remove, abolish, cancel, except
221 N3	222 N3
カン perfect, completion, end	お.りる お.ろす ふ.る ふ.り くだ.る コウ ゴ クダ. descend, precipitate, fall, surrender

223 N3	224 N3
責	捕

225 N3	226 N3
危	給

227 N3	228 N3
苦	迎

223 N3 せ.める セキ blame, condemn, censure	**224** N3 と.らえる と.らわれる と.る とら.える とら.われる つか.まえる つか.まる ホ catch, capture
225 N3 あぶ.ない あや.うい あや.ぶむ キ dangerous, fear, uneasy	**226** N3 たま.う たも.う キュウ -タマ. salary, wage, gift, allow, grant, bestow on
227 N3 くる.しい -ぐる.しい くる.しむ くる.しめる にが.い にが.る ク suffering, trial, worry, hardship, feel bitter, scowl	**228** N3 ゲイ ムカ.エ welcome, meet, greet

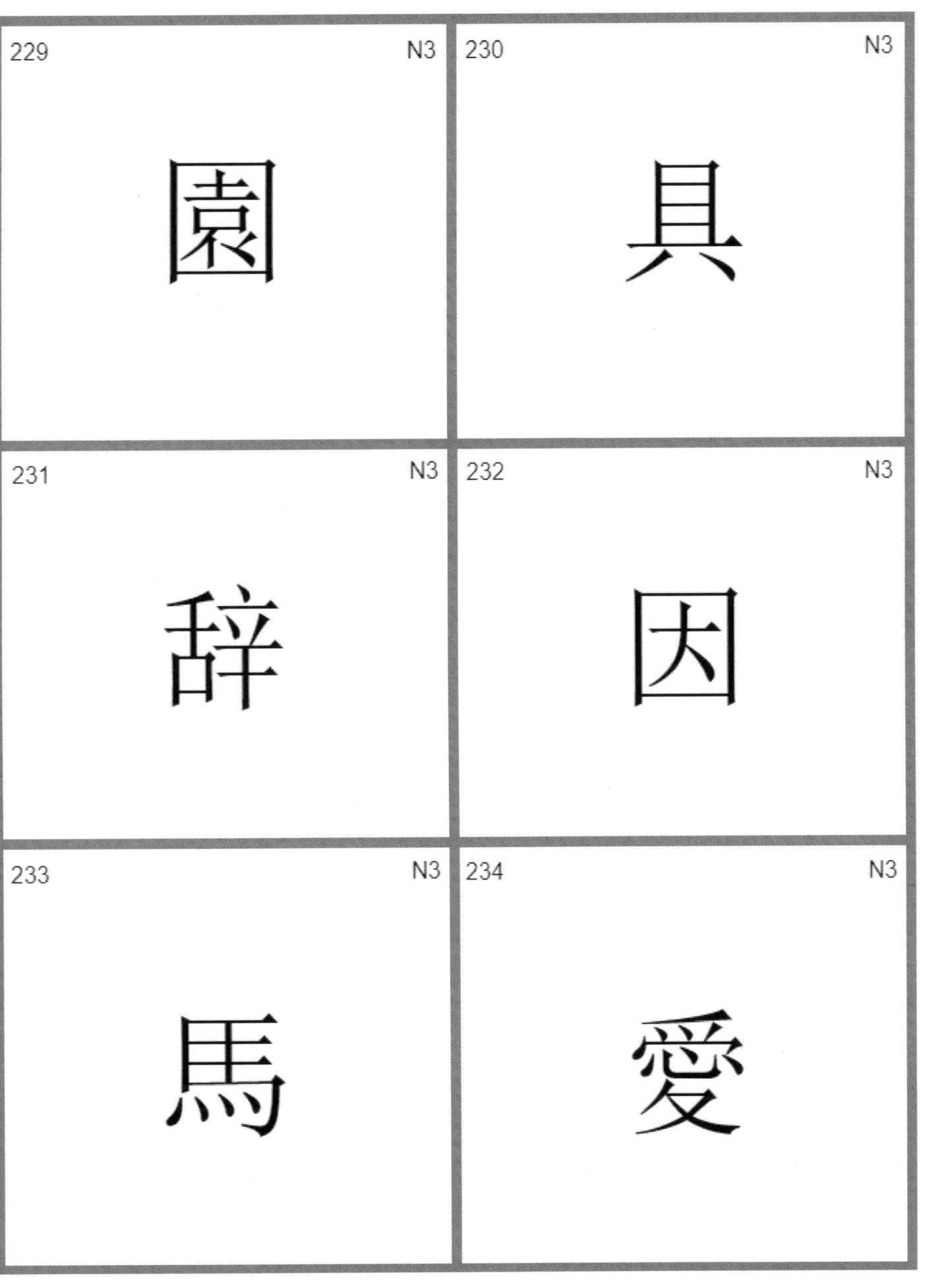

エン　ソ park, garden, yard, farm	そな.える　グ　ツブサ. tool, utensil, means, possess, ingredients, counter for armor, suits, sets of furniture
や.める　いな.む　ジ resign, word, term, expression	よ.る　イン　チナ. cause, factor, be associated with, depend on, be limited to
うま　うま-　バ horse	アイ　イト.シ love, affection, favourite

235 N3	236 N3
富	彼

237 N3	238 N3
未	舞

239 N3	240 N3
亡	冷

235 N3 と.む フ フウ ト wealth, enrich, abundant	236 N3 かれ かの ヒ カ. he, that, the
237 N3 いま.だ ま.だ ひつじ ミ ビ un-, not yet, hitherto, still, even now, sign of the ram, 1-3PM, eighth sign of Chinese zodiac	238 N3 ま.う -ま.う まい ブ dance, flit, circle, wheel
239 N3 な.い な.き- ほろ.びる ほろ.ぶ ほろ.ぼす ボウ モウ deceased, the late, dying, perish	240 N3 つめ.たい ひ.える ひ.や ひ.ややか ひ.やす ひ.やかす さ.める さ.ます レイ cool, cold (beer, person), chill

241 N3	242 N3
適	婦

243 N3	244 N3
寄	顔

245 N3	246 N3
類	余

241 N3	242 N3
かな.う テキ suitable, occasional, rare, qualified, capable	よめ フ lady, woman, wife, bride

243 N3	244 N3
よ.る -よ.り キ ヨ.セ draw near, stop in, bring near, gather, collect, send, forward	かお ガン face, expression

245 N3	246 N3
たぐ.い ルイ sort, kind, variety, class, genus	あま.る あま.り ヨ アマ. too much, myself, surplus, other, remainder

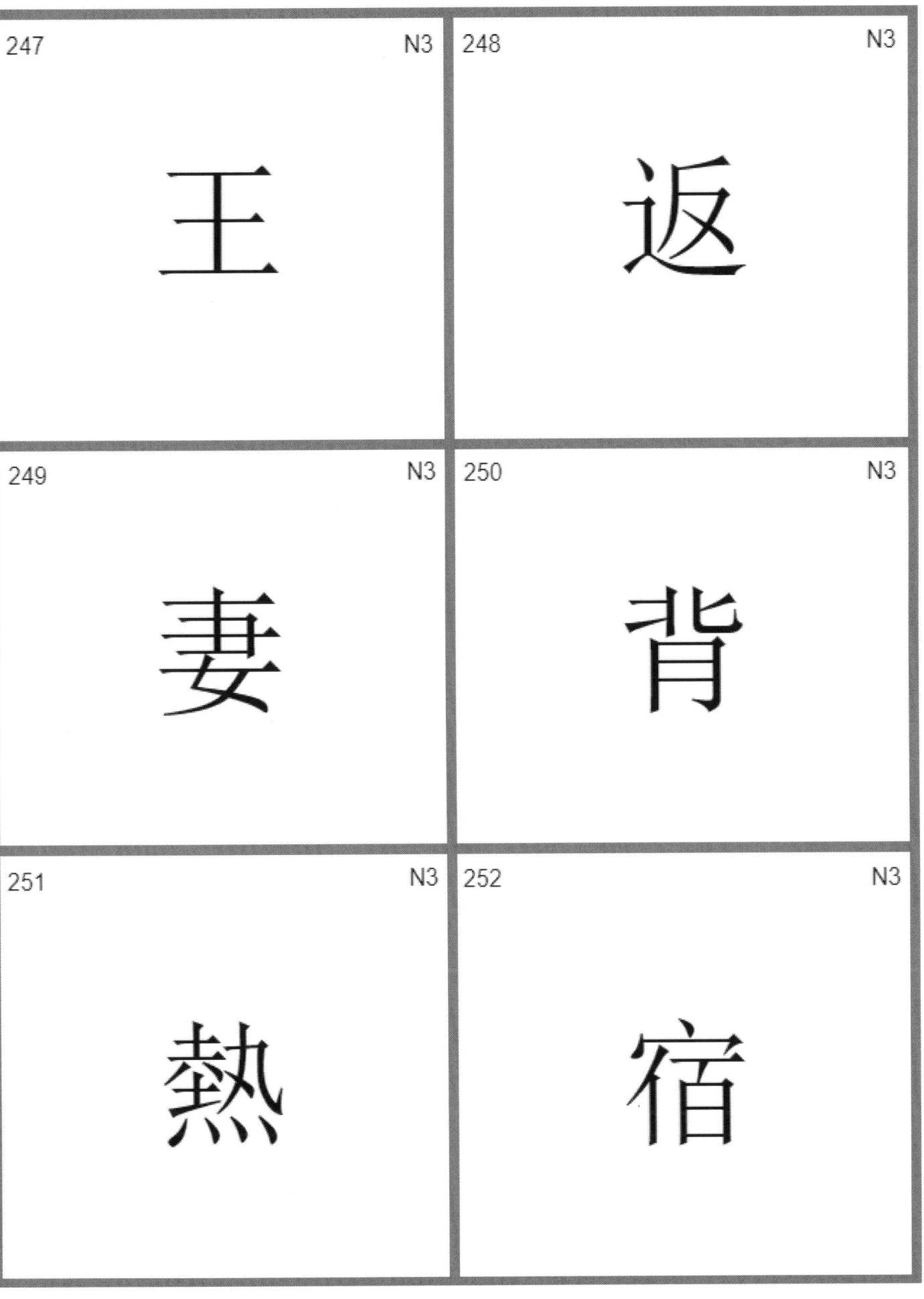

247 N3 オウ -ノ king, rule, magnate	248 N3 かえ.す -かえ.す かえ.る -かえ.る ヘン return, answer, fade, repay
249 N3 サイ ツ wife, spouse	250 N3 せ せい そむ.く そむ.ける ハイ stature, height, back, behind, disobey, defy, go back on, rebel
251 N3 ネツ アツ. heat, temperature, fever, mania, passion	252 N3 やど やど.る シュク ヤド. inn, lodging, relay station, dwell, lodge, be pregnant, home, dwelling

253 N3	254 N3
薬	険

255 N3	256 N3
頼	覚

257 N3	258 N3
船	途

253 N3 ヤク クス medicine, chemical, enamel, gunpowder, benefit	**254** N3 けわ.しい ケン precipitous, inaccessible place, impregnable position, steep place, sharp eyes
255 N3 たの.む たの.もしい ライ タヨ. trust, request	**256** N3 おぼ.える さ.ます さ.める さと.る カク memorize, learn, remember, awake, sober up
257 N3 ふね ふな セン ship, boat	**258** N3 みち ト route, way, road

259 N3	260 N3
許	抜

261 N3	262 N3
便	留

263 N3	264 N3
罪	努

259 N3 ゆる.す もと キョ permit, approve	**260** N3 ぬ.く -ぬ.く ぬ.き ぬ.ける ぬ.かす バツ ハツ ハイ ヌ.カ slip out, extract, pull out, pilfer, quote, remove, omit
261 N3 たよ.り ベン ビン convenience	**262** N3 と.める と.まる とど.める とど.まる リュウ ル ルウブ detain, fasten, halt, stop
263 N3 つみ ザイ guilt, sin, crime, fault, blame, offense	**264** N3 つと.める ド toil, diligent, as much as possible

265 N3	266 N3
精	散

267 N3	268 N3
静	婚

269 N3	270 N3
喜	浮

265 N3	266 N3
セイ ショウ シヤ refined, ghost, fairy, energy, vitality, semen, excellence, purity, skill	ち.る ち.らす -ち.らす ち.らかす ち.らかる サン バ scatter, disperse, spend, squander
267 N3	268 N3
しず- しず.か しず.まる セイ ジョウ シズ.メ quiet	コン marriage
269 N3	270 N3
よろこ.ぶ キ ヨロコ.バ rejoice, take pleasure in	う.く う.かれる う.かぶ む フ ウ.カベ floating, float, rise to surface

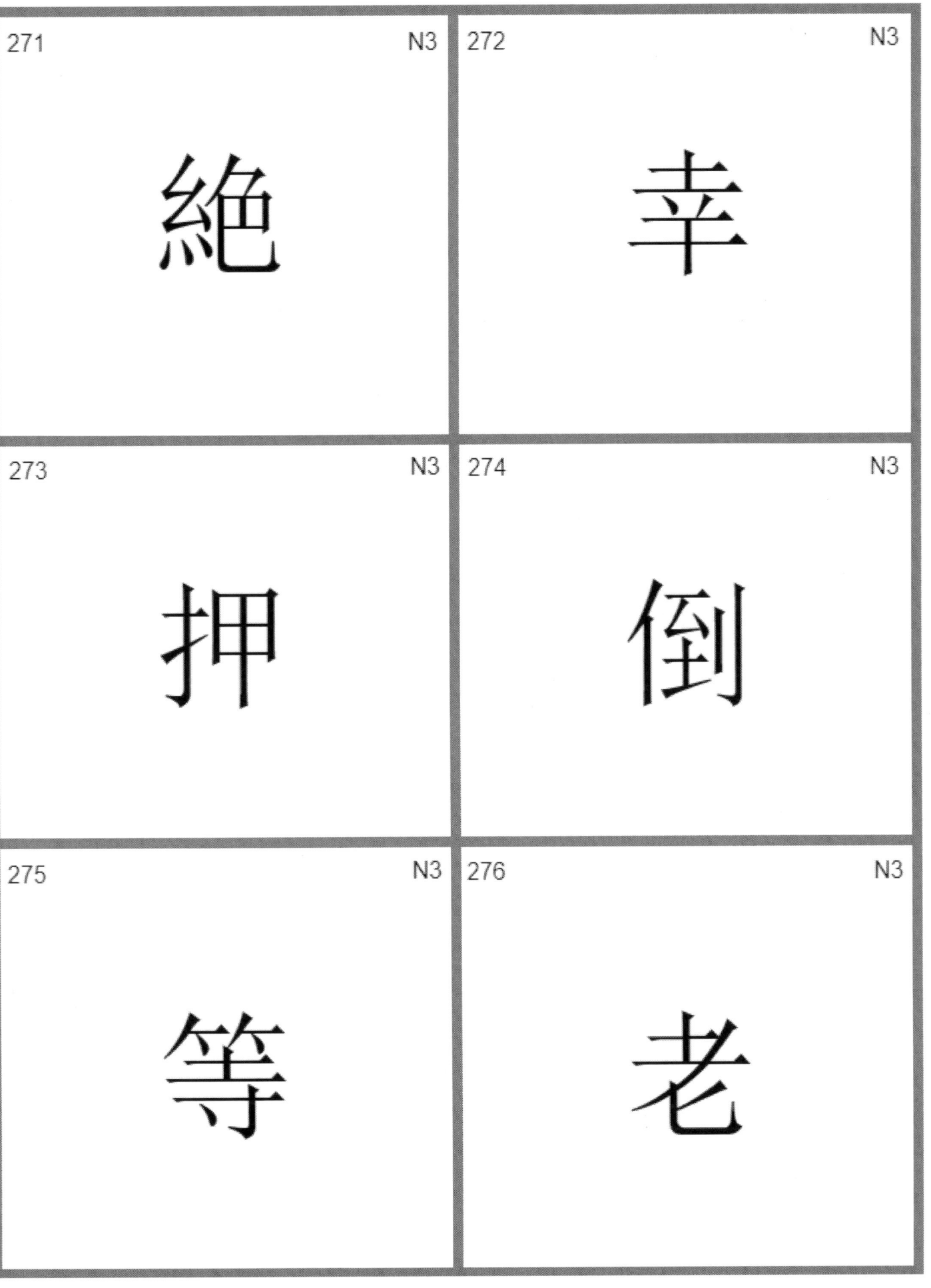

271 — N3
た.える た.やす た.つ ゼツ
discontinue, beyond, sever, cut off, abstain, interrupt, suppress

272 — N3
さいわ.い さち コウ シアワ.
happiness, blessing, fortune

273 — N3
お.す お.し- お.っ- お.さえる オウ オサ.エ
push, stop, check, subdue, attach, seize, weight, shove, press, seal, do in spite of

274 — N3
たお.れる -だお.れ たお.す トウ
overthrow, fall, collapse, drop, break down

275 — N3
ひと.しい など トウ
- etc., and so forth, class (first), quality, equal, similar

276 — N3
お.いる ロウ フ.ケ
old man, old age, grow old

277 N3	278 N3
曲	払

279 N3	280 N3
庭	徒

281 N3	282 N3
勤	遅

277 N3 ま.がる キョク マ.ゲ bend, music, melody, composition, pleasure, injustice, fault, curve, crooked, perverse, lean	**278** N3 はら.う -はら.い フツ ヒツ ホツ -バラ. pay, clear out, prune, banish, dispose of
279 N3 テイ ニ courtyard, garden, yard	**280** N3 いたずら ト ア junior, emptiness, vanity, futility, uselessness, ephemeral thing, gang, set, party, people
281 N3 つと.める -づと.め つと.まる いそ.しむ キン ゴン diligence, become employed, serve	**282** N3 おく.れる おく.らす チ オソ. slow, late, back, later

283 N3 居	284 N3 雑
285 N3 招	286 N3 困
287 N3 欠	288 N3 更

283 N3 い.る -い キョ コ オ. reside, to be, exist, live with	284 N3 まじ.える まじ.る ザツ ゾウ miscellaneous
285 N3 まね.く ショウ beckon, invite, summon, engage	286 N3 こま.る コン quandary, become distressed, annoyed
287 N3 あくび lack, gap, fail	288 N3 さら さら.に ふ.ける ふ.かす コウ grow late, night watch, sit up late, of course

289 N3	290 N3
刻	賛
291 N3	292 N3
抱	犯
293 N3	294 N3
恐	息

289 N3 きざ.む きざ.み コク engrave, cut fine, chop, hash, mince, time, carving	**290** N3 たす.ける たた.える サン approve, praise, title or inscription on picture, assist, agree with
291 N3 だ.く いだ.く ホウ カカ.エ embrace, hug, hold in arms	**292** N3 おか.す ハン ボン crime, sin, offense
293 N3 おそ.れる おそ.る おそ.ろしい こわ.い こわ.がる キョウ fear, dread, awe	**294** N3 いき ソク breath, respiration, son, interest (on money)

295 N3	296 N3
遠	戻

297 N3	298 N3
願	絵

299 N3	300 N3
越	欲

295 N3	296 N3
エン オン トオ. distant, far	もど.す もど.る レイ re-, return, revert, resume, restore, go backwards

297 N3	298 N3
ねが.う ガン -ネガ petition, request, vow, wish, hope	カイ エ picture, drawing, painting, sketch

299 N3	300 N3
こ.す -こ.す -ご.し こ.える エツ オツ -ゴ. surpass, cross over, move to, exceed, Vietnam	ほっ.する ほ.しい ヨク longing, covetousness, greed, passion, desire, craving

301 N3	302 N3
痛	笑
303 N3	**304 N3**
互	束
305 N3	**306 N3**
似	列

301 N3 いた.い いた.む いた.ましい いた.めるツウ pain, hurt, damage, bruise	**302** N3 わら.うショウ エ. laugh
303 N3 たが.い かたみ.にゴ mutually, reciprocally, together	**304** N3 たば たば.ねる つか つか.ねるソク bundle, sheaf, ream, tie in bundles, govern, manage, control
305 N3 に.るジ ヒ. becoming, resemble, counterfeit, imitate, suitable	**306** N3 レツ file, row, rank, tier, column

307 N3	308 N3
探	逃

309 N3	310 N3
遊	迷

311 N3	312 N3
夢	君

307 N3 さぐ.る さが.す タン grope, search, look for	308 N3 に.げる に.がす のが.す のが.れる トウ escape, flee, shirk, evade, set free
309 N3 あそ.ぶ ユウ ユ アソ.バ play	310 N3 まよ.う メイ astray, be perplexed, in doubt, lost, err, illusion
311 N3 ゆめ ゆめ.みる くら.い ム ボウ dream, vision, illusion	312 N3 きみ クン -ギ old boy, name-suffix

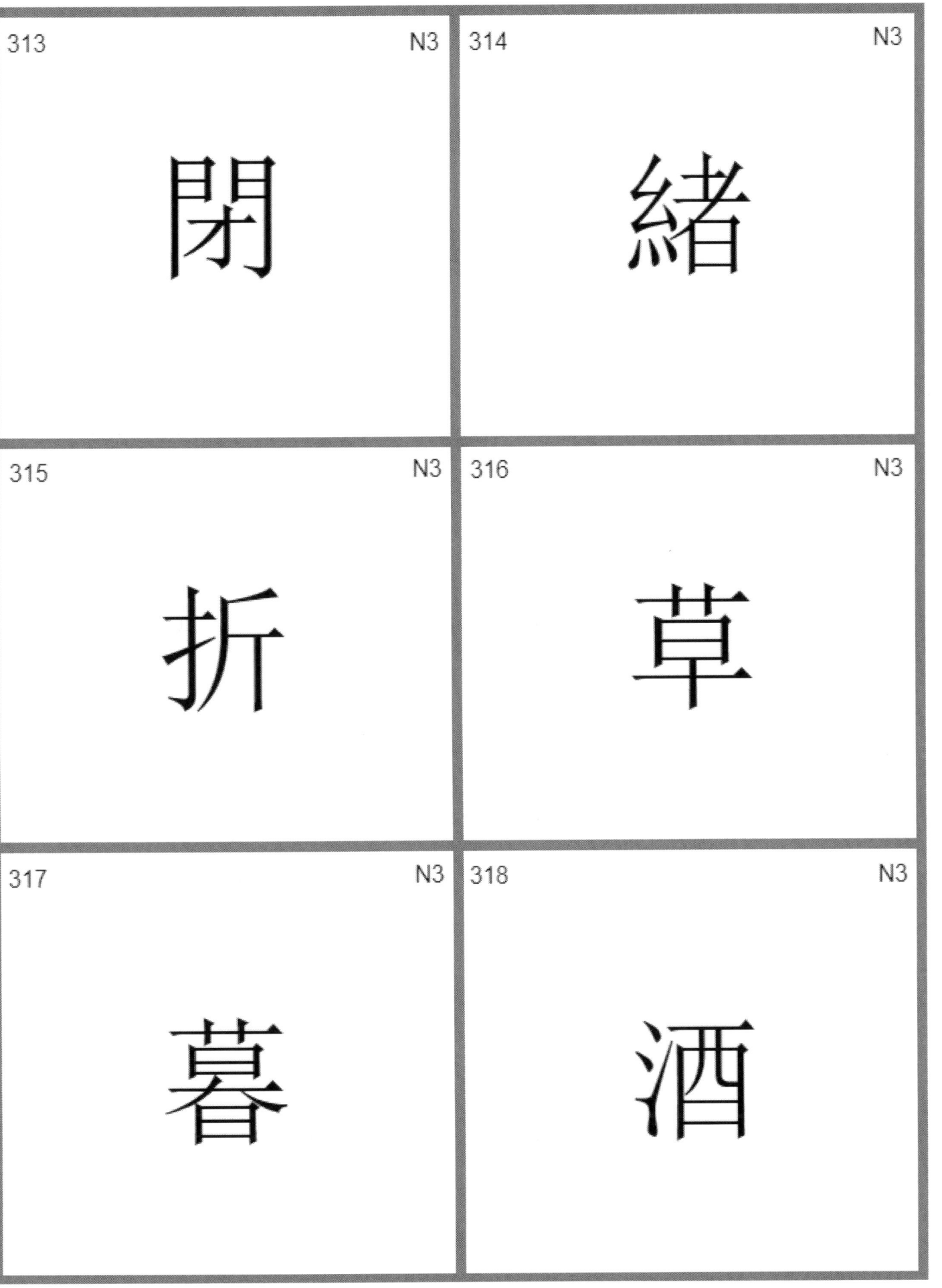

313 N3	314 N3
と.じる と.ざす し.める し.まる ヘイ タ.テ closed, shut	お ショ チョ イト グ thong, beginning, inception, end, cord, strap

315 N3	316 N3
お.る おり お.り -お.り セツ オ.レ fold, break, fracture, bend, yield, submit	くさ くさ- ソウ -グ grass, weeds, herbs, pasture, write, draft

317 N3	318 N3
く.れる ボ ク.ラ livelihood, make a living, spend time	さけ さか シュ sake, alcohol

319 N3	320 N3
悲	晴

321 N3	322 N3
掛	到

323 N3	324 N3
寝	暗

319 N3	320 N3
かな.しい かな.しむ ヒ jail cell, grieve, sad, deplore, regret	は.れる は.れ は.れ- -ば.れ セイ ハ.ラ clear up
321 N3	322 N3
か.ける -か.ける か.け -か.け -が.け か.かる -か.かる -が.かる か.かり -が.かり かかり カイ ケイ -ガ カ hang, suspend, depend, arrive at, tax, pour	いた.る トウ arrival, proceed, reach, attain, result in
323 N3	324 N3
ね.る ね.かす い.ぬ みたまや や.める シン lie down, sleep, rest, bed, remain unsold	くら.い アン darkness, disappear, shade, informal, grow dark, be blinded

325 N3	326 N3
盗	吸

327 N3	328 N3
陽	御

329 N3	330 N3
歯	忘

325 N3 ぬす.む ぬす.み トウ steal, rob, pilfer	326 N3 す.う キュウ suck, imbibe, inhale, sip
327 N3 ヨウ sunshine, yang principle, positive, male, heaven, daytime	328 N3 おん- お- み ギョ ゴ honorable, manipulate, govern
329 N3 よわい は よわ.い よわい.する シ tooth, cog	330 N3 わす.れる ボウ forget

331 雪	332 吹
333 娘	334 誤
335 洗	336 慣

331 N3 セツ ユ snow	**332** N3 スイ フ. blow, breathe, puff, emit, smoke
333 N3 むすめ こジョウ daughter, girl	**334** N3 あやま.る -あやま.るゴ mistake, err, do wrong, mislead
335 N3 セン アラ. wash, inquire into, probe	**336** N3 な.れる な.らすカン accustomed, get used to, become experienced

337 N3	338 N3
礼	窓

339 N3	340 N3
昔	貧

341 N3	342 N3
怒	泳

337 N3	338 N3
レイ ラ salute, bow, ceremony, thanks, remuneration	まど てんまど けむだし ソウ ス window, pane

339 N3	340 N3
むかし セキ シャク once upon a time, antiquity, old times	まず.しい ヒン ビン poverty, poor

341 N3	342 N3
いか.る おこ.る ド ヌ angry, be offended	およ.ぐ エイ swim

343 N3	344 N3
祖	杯

345 N3	346 N3
疲	皆

347 N3	348 N3
鳴	腹

343 N3 ソ ancestor, pioneer, founder	344 N3 さかずき ハイ counter for cupfuls, wine glass, glass, toast
345 N3 つか.れる -づか.れ つか.らすヒ exhausted, tire, weary	346 N3 みな カイ ミン all, everything
347 N3 な.く な.る メイ ナ.ラ chirp, cry, bark, sound, ring, echo, honk	348 N3 はら フク abdomen, belly, stomach

349 N3	350 N3
煙	眠
351 N3	352 N3
怖	耳
353 N3	354 N3
頂	箱

349 N3 けむ.る けむり エン ケム. smoke	350 N3 ねむ.る ミン ネム. sleep, die, sleepy
351 N3 こわ.い こわ.がる お.じる おそ.れる フ ホ dreadful, be frightened, fearful	352 N3 ジ ミ ear
353 N3 いただ.く いただき チョウ place on the head, receive, top of head, top, summit, peak	354 N3 はこ ソウ box, chest, case, bin, railway car

355 N3	356 N3
晚	寒

357 N3	358 N3
髪	忙

359 N3	360 N3
才	靴

355 N3 バン nightfall, night	356 N3 カン サム. cold
357 N3 ハツ カ hair of the head	358 N3 いそが.しい せわ.しい おそ.れる うれえるさまボウ モウ busy, occupied, restless
359 N3 サイ genius, years old, cubic shaku	360 N3 くつ カ shoes

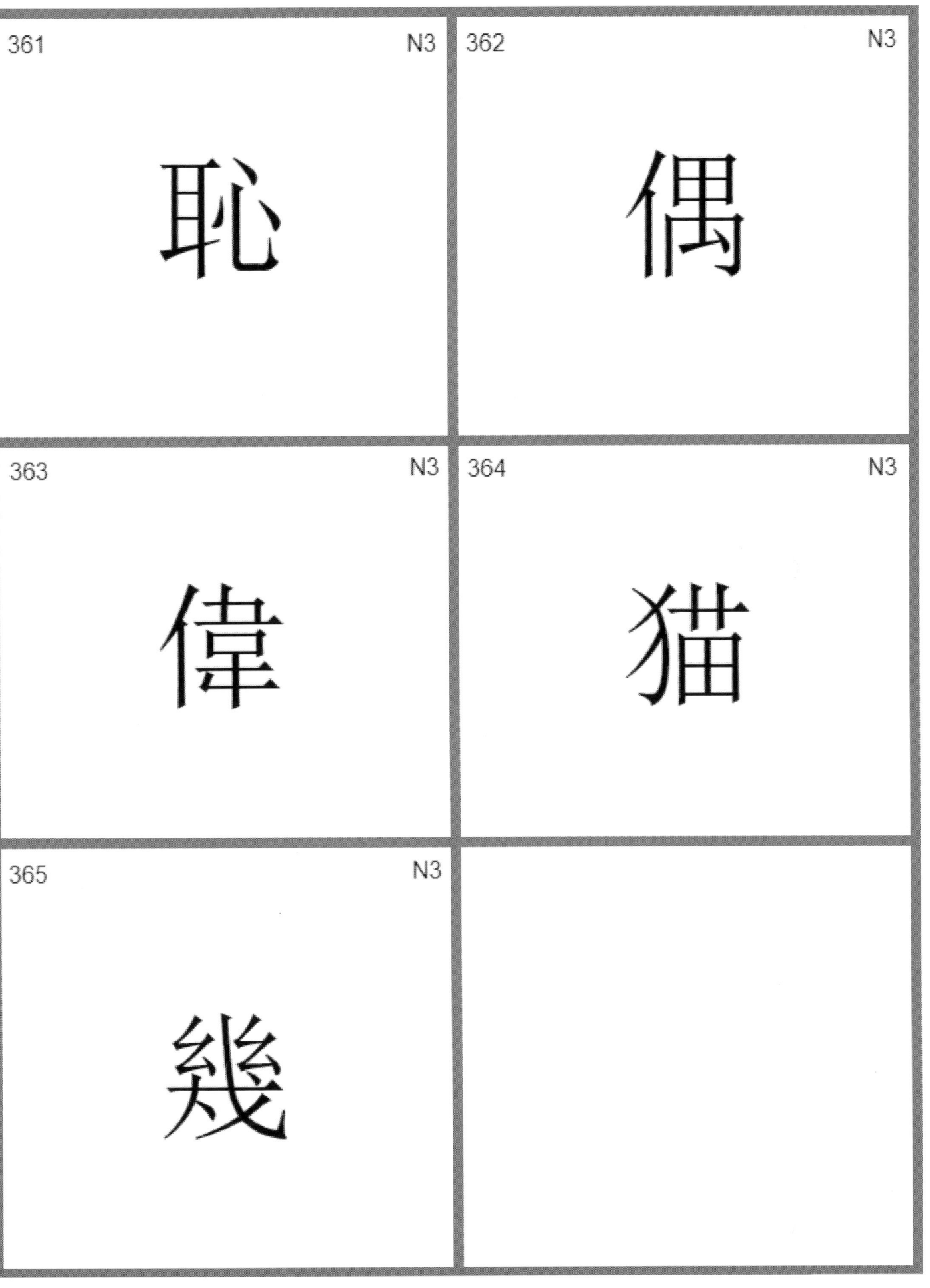

361　　　　　　　　N3 は.じる　はじ　は.じらう は.ずかしい チ shame, dishonor	362　　　　　　　　N3 たま グウ accidentally, even number, couple, man & wife, same kind
363　　　　　　　　N3 イ エラ. admirable, greatness, remarkable, conceited, famous, excellent	364　　　　　　　　N3 ねこ ビョウ cat
365　　　　　　　　N3 いく- いく.つ キ イク. how many, how much, how far, how long	

Made in the USA
Monee, IL
20 April 2021